Arundel (

A BRIEF HISTORY

The Parish Church of St Nicholas and the
Collegiate Chapel of the Blessed Trinity (Fitzalan Chapel)

Few town views in England can rival that of Arundel. For travellers journeying from the east or the south, it begins as a mere glimpse of a hill rising from the floodplain of the River Arun. Move closer, and you discover the commanding presence of the Roman Catholic Cathedral and imposing castle, with the comparatively retiring Anglican parish church nestled between them.

Arundel itself dates back to prehistoric days, and the early Britons certainly knew it; Romans built a villa here, while Saxons left evidence of their occupation. But the story of the present town only really developed after the Norman Conquest.

Within a year of the battle of Hastings (1066), Roger de Montgomery was granted about a third of Sussex by William I of Normandy. Instructed to defend his land effectively, Montgomery built a wooden castle in 1067. Today, after many rebuilds and enlargements, the castle is still occupied by Montgomery's descendants, from the Aubignys and the Fitzalans, through to the Howards, Dukes of Norfolk.

Before long, the town became the administrative and trading centre for a wide area. By 1300, Arundel had a port (licensed in 1071), a twice-weekly market, three fairs a year and two Members of Parliament. A defensive wall also surrounded the town.

Arundel

Arundel is shown on the 1360 Gough map on the pilgrimage route from Southampton to Canterbury. At this period maps were orientated toward Jerusalem with east at the top.

Arundel priests who died during the plague

The first outbreak

Robert de Stoke	1349
Walter de Flyttewyp	1349
William de Merton	1349
Williuam Dodynton	1350
Richard Bernard	1350

The second outbreak

William att Hull	1353
Adm de Lymberg	1354
Edmund de Cotton	1355

The First Church 1066–1380

The first stone church was built shortly after the Norman Conquest, as mentioned in the Domesday Book of 1086. It was built on the same site as the current church but was considerably smaller.

Along with an adjacent priory, the church was dedicated to St Nicholas, the patron saint of sailors, no doubt due to the port it overlooked.

It was linked to Sees Abbey in Normandy shortly after 1149, leading to the expulsion of 'evil-living clerics' and their replacement by monks chosen by the abbot. Thereafter it became a Benedictine priory.

The Church subsequently suffered a period of neglect and decline. This was due to two major fires in Arundel (1338 and 1344), the 'poverty of its possessors' and the Black Death in 1349, which claimed the lives of five priests and over half the population in just one year.

An absence of proper records from this time means that a total of 14 known priests are missing from the list of vicars in the church.

In 1354, Pope Innocent VI granted the 3rd Earl of Arundel permission to found a college of secular canons, which is to say a college of clergy who were not bound by a monastic rule. However, the Earl died before he could use the permission and it was left to his son, the 4th Earl, Richard, to implement his father's will and establish the college and church.

The New Church From 1380

Although the parish church and College were both built at the same time, the College was dedicated to the Holy Trinity while the church was dedicated to St Nicholas as before. They were built in the Gothic Perpendicular style, one of England's most valuable contributions to European architecture.

Two of the most celebrated master masons (or architects) of the day were almost certainly closely associated with the creation of Arundel's church and collegiate chapel. These were Henry Yeveley, who was also responsible for the nave of Canterbury Cathedral and the completion of the nave at Westminster Abbey, and the equally famed William Wynford, who rebuilt the great nave at Winchester Cathedral. Moreover, the collegiate chapel's vaulted timber roof was

St Nicholas Church and the College ruins after 1782. Although in ruins, the footprint and layout of the College is clearly visible.

probably created by the famous carpenter Hugh Herland, who collaborated with Wynford on the chapel at Winchester College.

The new church was built on a grand scale, as befitted the status of the castle and its earls. Nevertheless, this did not stop the builders from recycling a good deal of stone from the earlier building.

The exterior is largely built of flint with a mixture of stone, predominantly Pulborough Stone, quarried some 10 miles north of Arundel. This attractive combination was often arranged to create a loose chequer-work pattern. However, as was the case with many churches not faced with dressed stone, the outside walls may have been covered with several coats of lime render. At Arundel, even prior to the 1873-74

CONSECRATION CROSSES

These crosses, customarily painted in red within a red circle, are now comparatively rarely found within our churches. There would usually have been twelve inside the church and twelve outside. Their purpose was to celebrate the triumph of the Cross, the outward sign of Christ's victory, and to frighten demons. They were mostly painted on the walls around 8ft (2.5 metres) above the floor, as may be seen in Arundel today. Each interior cross had a bracket for a candle, which when lit together symbolised the ministry of the twelve Apostles. Today there remain just six (restored) interior crosses in St Nicholas Church.

THE PULPIT

The pulpit is in the style of Henry Yeveley as particularly evidenced by the dagger motif which also appears in his work in Winchester. Before about 1400 stone and wooden pulpits were rare as people stood in church while sermons were often given from the chancel, altar steps and even rood lofts. Only a few other medieval churches in England have a stone pulpit incorporated into the fabric of the building. The pulpit has had minor alterations over the years, including a period as a private pew followed by the Victorian addition of the lectern extension inscribed Revd George Hart 1859.

restoration, there was what was described as a 'rough coat on the exterior walls', which was scheduled to be removed before re-pointing.

The church has three porches, to the north, south and, unusually in medieval churches, the west. It is thought that the north and west entrances were mostly used at this time.

Moving to the interior, the church has a five-bay nave, some 38ft 9in high (11.77 metres) to the central ridge beam. Unusually high aisles end in tall arches that lead into curiously truncated transepts. The crossing pillars and arches cleverly combine to make the church appear larger than it really is. The nave pillars have four shafts and four hollows in the diagonals, and expert opinion suggests that they are made of Beer Stone (from eastern Devon), the arches themselves being made of Pulborough Stone, creating a subtle change in texture and colour.

A notable feature of Arundel's church is that the clerestory windows are essentially circular, something that can be found elsewhere in Sussex in the group of village churches at Beddingham, Piddinghoe and West Firle.

Another distinctive feature is the dagger motif above the arches of the pulpit and in most of the window tracery. This is similar to designs in the cloister windows at New College Oxford and Winchester College. Both these seats of learning were founded by William of Wykeham in 1380, the same year as the building of Arundel Church commenced.

The Sussex marble font dates from the building of the church. Its original location within the church is unclear, although traditionally fonts are found near the church's entrance. A plan shows that in the years immediately prior to 1874 it was located in the south transept.

Originally known as the parish or 'vicar's chancel', the south transept

Sussex marble font, 1380.

housed the 'parish altar'. Today it is the Lady Chapel.

Although currently hidden inside the organ, there is a piscina on the north side of the north-east crossing pillar, indicating that the north transept would also have housed an altar.

The thick corbels on either side of the chancel arch probably supported a large rood—a crucifix flanked by the Virgin Mary and St John set on a beam or in a loft. Access to this loft was via the same stairway that leads to the ringing chamber, belfry and tower parapet. A door can still be seen, perhaps indicating that the rood may have been above the loft rather than part of it.

The wrought-iron screen dividing the nave from the church's chancel, which housed the Collegiate Chapel, is almost certainly contemporary with the building. Its sheer size, delicacy and fine state of preservation is particularly remarkable. And since Sussex was a centre of the iron industry for centuries, it is perhaps appropriate to find such a screen in Arundel. Of note are the alternating lion's head and rosette stamps above the gate. The only other known example of lion's head badges are on fifteenth-century tomb railings at Canterbury.

The Church appears to have been largely finished by 1387. The Collegiate Chapel was dedicated on the Feast of Corpus Christi in the

Screen of Sussex wrought iron, 1380.

same year. However, the Lady Chapel, which is parallel to the chancel rather than to the east of the high altar, as is more customary, may not have been fully completed until around 1421, its exterior being more elaborate in comparison with the rest of the building.

MASONS' MARKS

The pillars of the church have a fine set of masons' marks recording the work of nine skilled men, each being the personal signature of the mason and cut into the stone before it left his work bench. The mark was usually awarded at the end of an apprenticeship when the fully trained craftsman was accepted into the masons' guild. Over a hundred have so far been recorded in Arundel church with many more hiding out of sight. There has been much debate as to their use. Two suggestions prevail, the most usual being that payment was made by the piece, although in the 14th century masons within the guild preferred to be paid by contract time. Alternatively, the marks may have been used by the overseers to check the quality of work produced by a particular mason. Or, there again, they may simply reflect the pride of the mason in his work.

A mark usually consisted of some three to five easily inscribed lines, but we have an unusual one in the form of a trefoil, being three small circles with a tail. This is the most prolific and appears on the more ornate scroll work at the base and capitals of the columns as well as on the pillars, and therefore might represent the work of a senior mason.

GRAFFITI

Close inspection of the pillars reveals a wealth of graffiti, much of it relating to the early years of the church when it was thought to be a way to protect against evil and invoke the intercession of the saints. Many of the meanings are now lost to us, but two symbols stand out as they appear in churches all over western Europe. Circles and their derivatives have long been thought to offer protective power, the most popular being the hexafoil or daisy wheel, at once deflecting major evil and attracting small malign influences to its lines which they were then doomed to follow for eternity. Appearing many times in the church, the double V is thought to be a devotion to the Virgin Mary and an invocation of her prayers. Both symbols survived the Reformation, leaving the church protected against witchcraft.

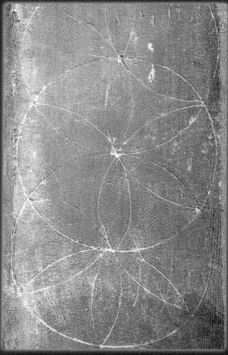

From 1500 to 1800

The three centuries from 1500 to 1800 marked a time of major upheaval and turmoil that re-shaped religious life in England.

The Reformation of the Church that swept through northern Europe from the 15th century had many causes, political and religious. New biblical interpretations on the nature of salvation, resentment of the power and wealth of the monasteries, along with a belief that the Church had become corrupt and was in need of spiritual reform, all had lasting consequences.

The English Reformation, which was perhaps as much political as religious, was ruthless and efficient, and set the agenda for all the major ecclesiastical change that followed. The passing of the Act of Supremacy in 1534 enabled Henry VIII to abolish Papal authority in England, becoming head of the English Church himself. The Act of Suppression followed in 1536, leading to the dissolution of the monasteries. Church wealth was confiscated on a huge scale between 1536 and 1540, largely, it would seem, to finance the king's debts. These enforced closures soon spread to the chantries and their chapels.

The winds of change were also felt in Arundel.

On 12th December 1544, almost on the eve of the abolition of the chantries, Henry Fitzalan, 12th Earl of Arundel, and godson of Henry VIII, voluntarily surrendered the chantry and College to the King. A few days later, on 26th December, the King granted the College along with all its endowments and goods back to the Earl for the payment of 1,000 marks and a yearly rent. The church's chancel and Collegiate Chapel thus became the Earl's private property and henceforth was used by him and his descendants as a family mausoleum, the purpose, of course, for which it had originally been founded.

Early in Queen Elizabeth I's reign a further burden was imposed on parishes with the Elizabethan Book of Homilies of 1571, obliging them to attend to 'the repairing and keeping clean, and comely adorning of churches'.

For many churches this would have been a financial burden. At Arundel the challenge must have been keenly felt as in 1579 it was also having to fund the costly repair of the nave roof (possibly also the west porch). In addition, parishes were burdened with the cost of removing the rood, often including the rood screen and loft where they existed,

Following the accession of the first Stuart king (James I) in 1603, a powerful High Church party emerged which encouraged a return to ritual, order and a concern for beauty and reverence. The chief proponent of this revival was William Laud, Archbishop of Canterbury (1633-45). He was much favoured by Charles I, and set about promoting his vision of the 'beauty of holiness'.

His Commissioner, Sir Nathaniel Brent, visited Arundel on 1st July 1635. His notes are not entirely clear, but it seems that he stipulated that the so-called 'vicar's chancel' was allowed to keep the rails around the altar, but that the chancel was only permitted to be used for the

Communion service and was to be kept locked at all other times.

Thomas Heyney was vicar of Arundel throughout this period. Appointed in 1620 he was expelled from his post in 1643 for his loose living and for being responsible for the appointment of 'scandalous persons to be placed for schoolmasters… to corrupt the youth'. His reputation for 'malignancie [sic] against the Parliament' could suggest that he might have been a Laudian sympathiser. He was followed by a succession of Puritan ministers.

Increasing tension between King and Parliament over several decades ultimately led to a bitter political, constitutional and religious power struggle and civil war in 1642.

Given the strategically important Royalist castle in their midst, the inhabitants of Arundel must surely have been aware of the possibility of military confrontation. Although captured by Parliamentarians in 1642, the castle was re-taken by Royalists in December the following year. However, under the command of General Waller, a superior Parliamentary force besieged the castle, finally forcing it to surrender

Imaginative depiction of Waller's occupation of the Fitzalan Chapel in 1643, painted in 1860 by Joseph Nash.

in January 1644, and its subsequent destruction in 1653.

The town also suffered severe damage. Town walls and gates were demolished and the old Marygate at the northern end of the town was 'shattered'. Waller's men stabled their horses in the Collegiate Chapel and tradition has it that they also used it for musket practice, seriously damaging the carvings, stained glass, bosses, corbels and the magnificent tombs.

Vandalism and destruction were widespread. All monuments of 'superstition and idolatry' were ordered to be removed from cathedrals, churches and chapels. It must have been a joyless time for those accustomed to the richness of medieval liturgy.

After the restoration of the Monarchy in 1660, there was a long period where local civic matters took precedence, meaning the church remained largely unaltered. From about this time, the Mayor and Burgesses agreed to pay half of the disbursements (expenses) of the church. This continued until about 1822, enabling the church to balance its books each year. The only major expenditure was the periodic painting of walls and repairs to the roof's leadwork.

ROYAL COAT OF ARMS

Royal Coats of Arms were introduced into English churches to trumpet Henry VIII's headship of the English Church as established by the Act of Supremacy (1534). After Henry's death in 1547 the Council of Edward VI took steps to see the removal of roods from rood lofts in churches and to replace them with the Royal Arms, something which became more or less obligatory upon Elizabeth's accession in 1558 and compulsory at the Restoration of the Monarchy in 1660.

The Arundel Arms is Hanoverian (though, unusually, neither king nor precise date are specified). It is, however, prior to 1800 as it contains the Fleur de lys, which was removed at the time of the union with Ireland in 1801. It has plainly been inserted in an older frame as the tails of both the lion and the unicorn have been cut off. It contains a signature of an H Wright 1854, who was a jobbing carpenter at that time and was paid £4.2s.6d. for "painting R. arms etc". This must have been a restoration.

CORBELS

These figures assist in the supporting of the roof beams. They are not normally found in village or even small town churches. Many in the Collegiate Chapel are quite sophisticated, especially those showing musicians and their instruments. The corbels in the nave of the Parish Church are rustic by comparison.

The corbel above the pulpit depicts the Green Man (3) which is the prechristian symbol of the rebirth that occurs every Spring. There is another Green Man in the Fitzalan Chapel under the nearest misericord.

The identity of the other corbel figures is unknown but the two at the west end are possibly King Edward III (1327–77) (1) and his wife Philippa (2) both of whom had close links to the Fitzalan Earls.

The Early Nineteenth Century

I t is not clear when the first pews and furniture were installed in St Nicholas, but the church plan at the Dissolution of the College (16th century) shows a complete lack of seating. It also shows altars only in the north and south transepts and a rood loft in the chancel arch.

We do know that the church was 're-pewed' by James Teasdale in 1818, so we can assume that the first pews were installed some time between 1600 and 1800. We also know that burials within the church ceased around 1800, perhaps because of the new pews and the re-laying of the ledger stones.

The pews installed in 1818 consisted of plain benches down the central aisle which were free for the use of the poor. The rest of the church was filled with box pews which were purchased or rented by the shop-keeping and merchant families of the town. There was a large square pew reserved for the Mayor and Corporation and another for their ladies (wives and daughters).

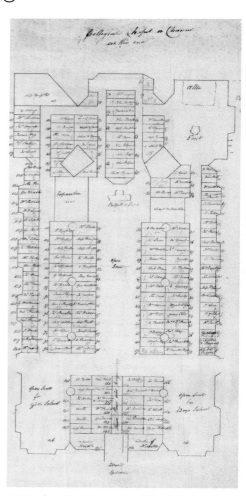

1843 plan showing ownership of the box pews.

Opposite: The new organ, pews and three-tier pulpit.

At various times, there were large pews at the back of the church for those in the Poor House, as well as pupils from the boys' and girls' schools.

Between 1844 and 1856, Henry, 13th Duke of Norfolk, who converted to Anglicanism in protest against the method of the restoration of the Roman Catholic hierarchy in England, took possession of two pews. He also paid for heating to be installed in 1852 and for a new set of eight bells in 1855. Interestingly, despite his earlier protestation, the 13th Duke converted back to Roman Catholicism upon his death-bed.

In 1823 galleries were introduced above the north and south aisles because 'the church does not have sufficient seats due to the increase of the population', taking the capacity up to 850. At a cost of £450, they were financed by six merchants who then sold or rented them at a profit.

It was about this time that a gothic three-tiered pulpit and reading desk was installed. However, this seems to have disappeared by the middle of the century and was replaced by a stone vicar's stall opposite the old pulpit. In 1856 hangings were purchased for the pulpit and in 1859 a reading desk was added.

The other important development was the installation of a new organ by William Gray in 1818. This was placed in the chancel arch. An organist was appointed at £30 a year and five or six singing boys were paid 10 shillings a year to sing at all services and attend a twice weekly practice.

There was a complete absence of stained glass until 1827 when Mayor Richard Holmes paid for the installation of a window depicting a

Swallow window, 1827.

18

swallow (Arundel's emblem) near the Corporation pew. Other stained-glass windows soon followed, mostly dedicated to leading citizens, until all plain windows were replaced by 1886. Similarly, the memorials on the walls virtually all date from the 19th century.

Gas lighting was installed in the church in 1853. An additional lamp was placed by the gate in 1863, and in the following year lighting was also added to the galleries.

Following the re-routing of the London Road from the north of the church to the south, a new path was laid to the south porch while the old path to the north was closed. At the same time, the Duke gave additional land to extend the churchyard to the south.

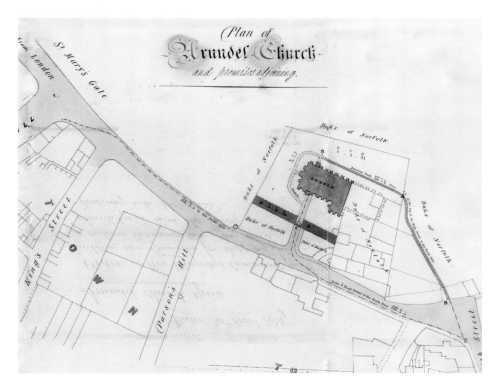

1847 map showing the new London Road, footpath to the south porch and the extension of the graveyard. It also shows the old path to the north porch.

WALL PAINTINGS

These depicted biblical stories, moral teachings or incidents in the lives of the saints. Sussex churches are rich in the remains of medieval wall paintings. The magnificent examples in nearby Hardham Church are amongst the earliest and were created very late in the 11th century. Those of the Arundel paintings that remain date from the building of the church. They are to be found on the north wall of the north aisle and depict the Seven Deadly Sins and the Corporal Works of Mercy (both 1380) and the Coronation of the Virgin (1430). The Arundel paintings were painted over during the Reformation then rediscovered around 1873, and were treated in 1914 with what is likely to have been a wax resin which, we now know, harmed the paintings. Between the late 1960's and early 2000's some conservation work was carried out. Much still needs to be done to reveal the paintings to their greatest advantage.

The Coronation of the Virgin Mary.

Burying the dead. Part of the series depicting the Seven Corporal Works of Mercy.

Opposite: 1860, showing the galleries, gas lighting and Vicar's new stone stall.

STAINED GLASS

In English churches stained glass goes back to the 1100's. That in both halves of the Church dates from the 19th century, from between 1827 and 1891. The Fitzalan Chapel has a splendid east window of 1891 by Hardman and designed by C.A.Buckler, inspired by early 15th century glass which once graced this window, and which was certainly destroyed by General Waller's troops in 1643.

St Nicholas Church also has a Hardman window showing the Transfiguration, but the finest two windows are by the leading firm of Meyer & Co., Munich. These are the west window of Christ the Good Shepherd commemorating Revd George Hart (Vicar 1844-73) and costing £450 raised in a month by the ladies of Arundel. He is also featured in the left panel carrying out a baptism. The other Meyer window is Faith, Hope and Charity in the south aisle. The first window, by Willement (1827), was given by Mayor Richard Holmes and depicts the Arundel swallow. It was next to the Corporation pew. There are two windows by Burlison and Grylls (St Nicholas and the Tompkins window) and four by the three Gibbs brothers.

The west window by Meyer & Co., Munich, 1873.

Re-ordering The Church 1873–1878

By the second half of the 19th century, it became clear that drastic re-ordering was required. It was observed that 'decency and order in the service was almost an impossibility', the nave aisles were 'choked up by galleries' and 'a nostrum of more than usual absurdity still rose in the middle composed of a pulpit flanked by matching tubs for the reader and the clerk', and the 'communion table (in the south transept) had become invisible from the main part of the church'.

Appointed in 1844, Revd George Hart was determined to correct these shortcomings and set about the planning and fundraising required. Sadly, Hart died in 1873 before completing his vision, leaving it to his curate, Revd George Arbuthnot, who succeeded as vicar, to complete the scheme.

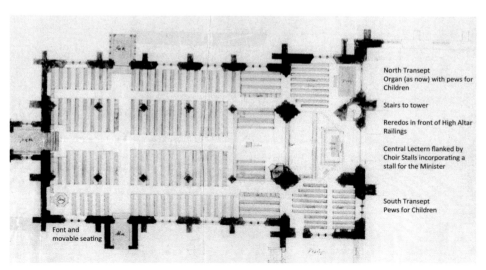

North Transept
Organ (as now) with pews for Children

Stairs to tower

Reredos in front of High Altar Railings

Central Lectern flanked by Choir Stalls incorporating a stall for the Minister

South Transept
Pews for Children

Font and movable seating

Sir George Scott's 1873 re-ordering plan.

Under the authority of the Bishop of Chichester, Richard Durnford, a licence was granted to 'perform Divine Service in the School Room during the time the Church is closed for restoration'.

Sir George Gilbert Scott, a leading church architect of the time, was appointed to plan and supervise the work, transforming the church from its medieval form to the layout that still largely survives to this day.

The galleries were removed, new oak pews replaced the old box pews and benches, and the organ was moved from the chancel arch to the north transept, with the original William Gray case replaced by one specially designed and installed by William Hill.

A chancel was created, surrounded by a low wall and gates. Within it was an altar and reredos designed by Fellowes Prynne. There were also choir and clergy stalls by Robinson of High Holborn and floor tiles by William Godwin & Sons of Lugwardine, Herefordshire.

A new clock by John Smith & Sons of Clerkenwell was installed in the tower in 1878 at a cost of about £200.

The new chancel, with choir stalls, altar and surrounding wall.

24

The work also included repairs to the roof, pillars, doorways and walls, including removing the accumulated earth outside them.

The Font was moved from the south transept to near the south entrance while other work was included 'to relay the old monumental slabs in their original position, remove the rough coat on the exterior and generally put the building into a complete state of repair'.

Although the church was re-dedicated on 24th September 1874, the work continued for some years after. Once completed, the finances were left in a poor state, prompting the introduction of weekly collections in 1878. But even then, an annual appeal was needed to balance the books.

CLOCK

There is evidence of a clock in the Church in the 17th century when for 200 years regular payments were made to local craftsmen for repair and maintenance. A decision was made to replace the old clock as part of the 1873–8 re-ordering and in November 1878 an order was placed with John Smith & Sons of London for a Turret Quarter Clock at a cost of £193-3-0 'including labour at 12/- per day'.

The Twentieth Century

Despite recent renovations, an invasion of deathwatch beetles meant the 19th century ended with major repairs to the nave roof. Combined with the ongoing cost of Scott's re-ordering, the church entered the 20th century seriously short of funds. This led to accusations by successive vicars that they were not receiving sufficient support from the congregation and subsequently a turnover of six vicars in just thirty years (1887–1917), two of whom only stayed for three years. Fortunately, the arrival of Revd Charles Winn in 1917 heralded twenty years of much-needed stability, as well as consolidating the church's increasingly High Church tradition.

After the reordering of the 1870s, the layout and furnishings of the church remained unaltered for over seventy years.

In 1951 a carved rood in stone by Clothilde Heighton was placed where the medieval rood loft had stood in the chancel arch. It depicted Christ flanked by the Blessed Virgin Mary and St John the Evangelist.

The rood above the high altar in 1951.

In 1977, during the week of Prayer for Church Unity, the iron grille and glass screen were opened for the first time in 433 years for an ecumenical service to be held in both parts of the church building. In order to open the gates the rood had to be taken down. Today it is located in the north churchyard.

The gates have been opened nine times since then, including for the funeral of Lavinia, Duchess of Norfolk, an Anglican, in 1995 and a Service of Commemoration in November 2018 to mark the 100th anniversary of the end of the First World War.

In 1977, there was a radical reordering of the sanctuary in keeping with the fashion of the time. The high altar was brought forward and the choir stalls put in its place. The Victorian wall surrounding the chancel was demolished and replaced by a simple rail, and the whole area was raised on a wooden platform and carpeted. This was followed by the erection of a west gallery, gallery room, kitchen, toilets and meeting room complex between 1981 and 1985.

There was a further re-ordering of the chancel in 1999, involving the restoration of the Godwin floor tiles, the re-siting of the choir stalls in the side aisles, moving the high altar back to its proper position and the introduction of a nave altar.

In 2007, the central section of the west gallery was removed giving more room for baptisms, exhibitions and concerts.

Other recent introductions have included various memorials and embellishments, including a new floor, doors and steps to the south porch in memory of Lavinia, Duchess of Norfolk (1999); the re-ordering of the Lady Chapel in memory of Rosalind Toole-Mackson in 2002, with furnishings by Katie Walker of Cox Farm Studios, Wareham; and the installation of the engraved inner glass doors of the west porch, designed by Melanie Howse and erected in memory of Jasmine Nash in 2009.

Icon of our Lady and the Christ Child with St Nicholas and St Richard of Chichester.

In 2015, an embroidered tapestry of the Burning Bush by Belinda Scarlett was introduced into the church, and in 2022, an icon of Our Lady and the Christ Child with St Nicholas and St Richard by Barbara Klimezuk-Moezulska was installed in the Lady Chapel in memory of Canon Brian Cook.

BELLS

Six new bells were hung in the tower in 1712. In 1840 came the commissioning of what seems to have been a clock bell, and an 1840 engraving of the exterior of the Church shows it hanging over the clock dial. It survived in this position for well over 100 years.

At least four of the 1712 bells survived for nearly one and a half centuries, the tenor cracking in 1829, it was said, whilst it was being rung for the Duke of York's funeral: another suffered the same fate a few years later.

In 1855, following a long silence, eight new bells by C & G Mears replaced the old ring. They were given by Henry, 13th Duke, and Charlotte, Duchess of Norfolk, and were opened by a band of the Ancient Society of College Youths on 25th October. These bells rang for the last time in December 1938 owing to the unsafe condition of the old wooden frame and the bells were stored in the Church. In 1950 the bells were rehung, retuned and placed in a new iron frame by Messrs Gillett and Johnston. The reinstated bells were rung again on 17th June 1950.

The Fitzalan Chapel

The Fitzalan Chapel, which occupies the church's chancel, was the chapel of the College of the Holy Trinity. Built between 1380 and 1387, it formed part of the larger project that included the church as a whole, the adjacent College buildings (dormitory, refectory, kitchen and Master's house) and the Hospital of the Holy Trinity (Maison Dieu), a shelter for the poor, sick and probably the many pilgrims that passed through Arundel.

The College's chapel was separated from the church's nave by the iron screen that exists to this day. It was a very common arrangement in medieval churches, separating the sacred side of the building used by the clergy, from the nave that housed the people.

The College was not a monastery, that is its clergy did not live by a monastic rule. Rather, the focus of the College's liturgical life was to act as a chantry, praying for the souls of its benefactors.

The College thrived, particularly in

Adam Eartham, first Master of the College.

the Middle Ages when it became a centre for the composition and performance of choral music. This led to the production of the Arundel Choir Book in about 1520, containing works by the notable composers Robert Fayrefax and Nicholas Ludford. This is one of only three medieval choir books that have survived to this day, the others being at Eton College and Caius College, Cambridge.

The College was occupied by thirteen chaplains, two deacons, two sub-deacons, two acolytes and four choristers.

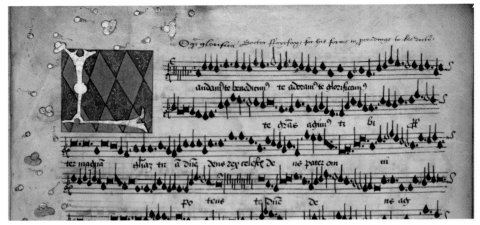

The Arundel Choir Book, c. 1520.

The College's clergy also supervised parish business, elected one of their number to act as vicar of the parish, another to take charge of the Hospital, and involved themselves in the life of the town.

This co-existence continued peacefully until the reign of Henry VIII (1509-47). As a result of his dispute with the Pope over his desire to divorce Catherine of Aragon, he passed the Act of Supremacy (1534), appointing himself as head of the church in England. This was followed by the Act of Suppression in 1536 to allow him to dissolve the monasteries and confiscate their wealth. This was later extended to the chantries. But before this could happen in Arundel,

Henry Fitzalan, 12th Earl of Arundel, surrendered the chapel and College to the King, before buying them back a week later in December 1544. From then on, the iron screen divided the Anglican parish church of St Nicholas from the privately owned chapel.

Sadly, the chapel was badly damaged during the Civil War (1642-49) and suffered even more from neglect during the absence of the Dukes of Norfolk over the following 150 years, culminating in the destruction of the original carved timber roof in 1782.

Various repairs were made during the 19th century, but the major restoration work was carried out from 1886 by Henry Fitzalan-

Opposite: The Fitzalan Chapel showing the Hardman window and the tomb of the Fifth Earl.

Howard, 15th Duke of Norfolk, to the plans of C. A. Buckler.

The masonry and wood carving were executed by Messrs Rattee and Kent of Cambridge in 1891, and to this day their work is an exemplary piece of restoration. In the same year, the installation of the east window was completed by Hardman and celebrated by a Mass for Duchess Minna, the Duke's mother. The window shows the Holy Trinity at its apex, while the lights below depict the ancestors of the 15th Duke in heraldic or contemporary dress.

This restoration came after a dispute in 1872 in which the Vicar and Churchwardens of St Nicholas

The chapel before it was restored.

claimed the chapel as the true chancel of the church.

They cited the years of neglect and lack of use by the Dukes and threatened to re-unite the chapel with the church.

The Duke responded by filling the arch with a solid brick wall. The Vicar, Revd George Arbuthnot, deliberately removed some of the bricks from the wall and a lawsuit became inevitable.

Revd George Arbuthnot, Vicar of Arundel 1873–79.

In 1879 Lord Chief Justice Coleridge found that the chapel was an independent ecclesiastical structure and not part of the Parish Church. Arbuthnot promptly resigned his post, taking instead the position of Vicar of Stratford upon Avon.

The wall remained in place until 1956, when Bernard Fitzalan-Howard, 16th Duke of Norfolk, removed the top half. In 1969 the church's council paid for the remainder of the wall to be removed and the erection of a new glass screen to fill the whole arch.

Although the chapel contains great treasures, the major artistic interest lies primarily in the tombs of the Earls of Arundel and Dukes of Norfolk, which form one of the finest assemblages of their kind in England.

There is also a fine set of corbels, mostly depicting angels with musical instruments, and 14th century canons' stalls, with one misericord hiding a Green Man.

The ornate tomb just below the altar is for Thomas Fitzalan, 5th Earl of Arundel, and his wife, surrounded by twenty-eight priests, symbolic of the Canons of the College. This was the first tomb placed in the chapel.

The tomb nearest to the screen in bronze commemorates Henry Fitzalan-Howard, 15th Duke of Norfolk (1847-1917), who not only restored the chapel, but built the Catholic parish church (now Arundel Cathedral) and rebuilt the castle.

The wall between the Church and Fitzalan Chapel, breached in July 1877 by Revd Arbuthnot.

ORGAN

This instrument, first built in 1817 by the well known London firm of William Gray & Son, estimated to cost £650, ultimately had three manuals, and was provided with an imposing neo-Gothic double case, facing west. With 22 speaking stops, this was a sizeable organ for its day. Thomas Bennett. organist of Chichester Cathedral, came over to open the organ on Sunday 10th August, bringing with him his choir to perform 'an appropriate service'. Only 13 churches in the entire diocese by then had organs (excepting barrel organs), and these were to be found in Chichester (seven), Lewes (two), Arundel, Lindfield, Brighton and Horsham (one each).

An early Arundel organist who stayed nearly 30 years was William Calkin (1820-49). He was elected a Member of the Royal Society of Musicians in 1819 and played regularly in the Theatre Royal in Drury Lane.

Fashionable alterations were carried out on the instrument in 1864 by Joseph P Walker, who added a full compass pedal stop. Ten years later the whole organ was rebuilt by Messrs J.M.& C.Corps of London, and moved to its present position on the floor of the north transept. The splendid case was destroyed. In 1878 new and colourful cladding was added by William Hill and Son, and electric blowing was introduced during 1949.

Apart from this little was done to the instrument between1878 and 1990, save for an occasional cleaning. Edward Bartlett (organist of Arundel from 1875-1920) wished for changes but, owing to a shortage of funds, precious little was achieved. J.W.Walker & Sons" eventual major overhaul in 1991 was essentially an historic restoration.

Shadows of the Past

Everywhere one looks in an ancient church there are shadows of those who went before us. Here we highlight two such 'shadows'.

Above the statue in the Lady Chapel is a curious monument that tells the all-too-familiar story of life cut short. It is sacred to the memory (M.S.) of L.D.P., who died in December 1823. A little research reveals that Lawrence Duprey Parsons was just a year old when his parents brought his body to the church for burial. They chose a poignant Latin epitaph that tells of their hope of heaven for their baby boy. An English translation reads: *Innocent and blessed, like a flower I fell and sleep. Traveller, why art thou sad? Happier I than you who weep.*

Our next shadow is harder to find. On the pillar by the lectern the name of Humfre Hyggon(s) is scratched into the stone, perhaps accompanied by a cheeky self-portrait.

Who was he? Thanks to the work of local researcher, Yvette Cook, we can add some colour to a name.

Humfre Higgons was the youngest brother, or perhaps half-brother, of the Master of the College, Dr Edward Higgons. He was taken on as a clerk and 'singing man' when his brother arrived in Arundel in 1520.

At times Humfre had to be reprimanded for his behaviour. He was chastised for talking during the daily services, drawing his sword against the precentor and 'riotous behaviour' in the town.

However, apart from his name scratched in stone, it is possible that Humfre left us something of real beauty – the Arundel Choirbook. There is evidence to suggest that it may have been created by his skilled hand.